Let's Get Talking

Exciting ways to help children with speech and language difficulties

ACKNOWLEDGEMENTS

Written by: Michael Jones & Jo Belsten

Illustrated by: Peter Scott

Published by: Lawrence Educational
Unit 21, Brookvale Trading Estate,
Birmingham B6 7AQ

ISBN: 978-1-903670-88-0

The authors wish to thank the following settings for their help with this publication and the photographs:

Downside Pre School, Luton
Smarteez Neighbourhood Nursery, Bedford
The Oaks Pre-school, Great Hollands, Bracknell, Berks
Greenside Nursery & Children's Centre, Luton
New Scotland Hill, Foundation Stage Class, Bracknell ,Berks
Foxhill Foundation Stage Class, Bracknell, Berks

CONTENTS PAGE

Introduction

This book provides fun ideas to improve the communication skills of children with speech and language difficulties in early years settings, in the first years of school, and also older children with additional learning needs. They can be used as part of everyday routines, as well as activities you can share individually, in pairs and in small groups.

How to use this book

We hope that the activities in this book will benefit *all* children's communication. You can try out these activities with children on their own, and gradually introduce other children so that they are learning and talking with each other in a group. Gradually build up a repertoire of games that children enjoy so that your communication groups really swing!

On many of the pages there are ideas for 'simple', 'harder' and 'extension' activities. These are designed to include all children, whatever their levels of speech and language difficulty.

A quick word about groups

Children with speech and language difficulties can find learning in a group particularly challenging. When planning who should be in your group, it is helpful to have a mixed group of children: some with well-developed communication as well as children who will need extra help.
The maximum number in a group should be between six and 10 children.

If you are sitting in a circle, always start with the child on your left-hand side and take turns clockwise. This helps children understand about taking turns. You may want to start with the most confident child, and place children with speech and language difficulties about third or fourth. That way they will have a good idea of what they need to do, and it will encourage their involvement.

Good talkers need:

- Confidence
- Something interesting to talk about
- Conversations
- Routine
- Good hearing
- Good well-being
- Rhyming and singing!

How do children learn to talk?

By answering this question we can understand what we can do to help children who are finding talking difficult.

All children, from birth onwards, need to have experiences that are interesting and make sense to them. They share these experiences with adults and other children and they particularly enjoy sharing activities with children who are already good talkers. Adults take time to listen to what they have to say, to answer children's questions, and point out new information that relates to their interests. What we are really describing are the ingredients of a good *conversation*: whether with children or between adults! Conversation is one of the main keys to all language learning. To have a good conversation, whether with babies or older children, we need to take *time* to listen to children, and help them listen and talk to each other.

Conversation is also about taking turns, and adults who are able to help children do this are also helping their social development. Young children learn to take turns first of all in play, and this gives them the skills they need to take turns in conversation. All children need lots of practice with talking in groups, listening, and taking turns when talking. Children with speech and language difficulties can take a little longer to learn the rules we expect in conversation, e.g. taking turns when talking, sharing the same topic, waiting, and listening.

Children also need to develop the *confidence* to use talk in order to communicate with adults and other children, especially when in groups in settings and school. This confidence comes from having lots of success in making yourself understood, and knowing that adults will give you time to say what you mean, and do their best to understand what you are saying, however you may be communicating.

Young children learn to talk quickest when they have a predictable *routine* which helps them make sense of their day. They need to be involved in talk as part of this routine and during everyday activities, e.g. when getting dressed, sharing meals, and playing outdoors. It is important for young children, and especially those with speech and language difficulties, to know what is going to happen next. Children need to be involved with lots of repetitive language, and encouraged to practice saying new words and sounds. When children learn songs and rhymes, they are building up their knowledge and use of speech sounds. Sharing books is very important for encouraging children's understanding, expressive language skills, and vocabulary.

As children's language develops, they like to talk about what they know. It is particularly important to make strong links with the families of children with speech and language difficulties, as they might have more difficulty telling you what they know about or are interested in.
Sometimes children with speech difficulties may have problems with learning to read and spell. One possible reason for this is weak *phonological awareness*. In other words it takes them longer to understand that words have patterns, can rhyme, and are made up of different sounds. For this reason, rhyming and singing become all the more important.

Let's talk about communication: some definitions

Communication

We communicate in lots of ways in order to share our messages and to understand each other: most often by the use of words, sounds, gestures, body language and symbols such as writing. When learning to communicate, young children initially use gestures. Over time these become supplemented and eventually dominated by words.

Some children with speech and language difficulties are able to use different ways to communicate, such as gestures and sign language, and can be very sociable. Others find it extremely difficult to get their message across, and this can lead to huge amounts of frustration.

It is helpful to think of ***language*** as being in three parts:

Understanding language (sometimes known as *comprehension*) – being able to work out what someone means when they talk to you. Young children gradually build up their understanding of words and meanings by hearing words used meaningfully over and over again. Gradually they are able to listen to longer sentences and new words in different situations, particularly when they first go to preschool, nursery or school. Some children with speech and language difficulties need extra support with understanding language.

Expressive language is the way that we convey our thoughts, ideas and feelings so that others can understand us: usually through words and sentences. It is very important to have a wide *vocabulary*: the words that we use in our language to name and describe objects and people in our world, and how we feel. By the age of three, many children understand thousands of words and use them regularly to make simple sentences. Children with expressive language difficulties find it hard to find the right words to say what they mean. They often have difficulties with using conjunctions, small grammatical words that are the links in sentences such as 'and',' but', and 'then'.

Speech (also known as *pronunciation* and *articulation*) is the expression of a message through the use of sounds. We use sounds to construct words. Children's speech develops gradually from babbling as babies to eventual clear individual words and sentences. Some children can take a long time to master all of the sounds of their language, and this might even continue into adulthood.

When children need help with speech and language

Language delay

This is when a child is taking longer than other children to understand and use words and sentences. They are, however, going through the stages you would normally expect – only later.

Children with language delay find it difficult to listen to people talking, especially in large groups. Their vocabulary is often limited, making it difficult to describe things, explain their ideas, and answer questions. Generally, children with language delay sound like those who are much younger. For example, a four-year-old with language delay may say, "Me no like that", as opposed to, "I don't like it because it is blue and my favourite colour is purple!"
Sometimes children with language delay need help to work out social rules in play and conversation – in particular taking turns in games and when speaking.

There is a wide variation in how fast different children develop speech and language. Many who cause their parents concern catch up quickly once they attend early years settings where there is plenty to talk about, adults with time to chat with them, and children with well-developed language which whom to play and talk.
Language delay can be caused by difficulties with a child's hearing and it is essential that everyone is aware if children are hearing well or not. If you and the family have concerns, then together seek advice from a Speech and Language Therapist.

Specific language difficulties

These are speech and language difficulties that are not just delayed, nor can they be explained because the child has a medical difficulty such as hearing loss, or a developmental difficulty, e.g. autism. These can be long term difficulties that need specialist support.

Younger children with specific language difficulties often appear to have a delay, but as they get older, their language and communication skills do not follow the normal patterns of development. They may have particular difficulty with understanding what people say. These difficulties can have a huge effect on their social, emotional and educational progress.

Speech sound delay

Whereas some children's speech is clear from a very young age, others can take much longer. Children can often say a sound on its own but take longer to use the sound in words. Children with language delay can also have delayed speech development. There may be no clear cause for some children to have speech delay. However, many children with hearing problems have delayed speech so it is essential to make sure that children with speech delay are hearing well.

Sometimes children with delayed speech sounds have difficulty with *phonological awareness.* This includes rhyming, understanding that rhyming patterns sound alike, and that the words we say are made up of different sounds. They may find it harder to tune into the rhythm and patterns in words, so extra support in singing, rhyming and listening can help, especially when it is part of a normal routine and with other children.

It is possible that some children facing early difficulties with speech sounds might also experience reading and spelling difficulties when they are older. This may be due to weak *phonological awareness.* It may also occur in families who have a history of reading and writing difficulties or confirmed dyslexia. Not every young child with speech sound delay will go on to have reading and spelling difficulties, but the support we give them early on will make sure that they develop firm foundations for literacy when they are older.

Speech disorder

Sometimes a child's speech is so difficult to understand that even their family struggle to make sense of what is being said. Occasionally, a child will have severe difficulties with co-ordinating his lips and tongue to achieve the correct place in the mouth at the right time. This is sometimes called *verbal dyspraxia.*

Very occasionally, a child has extreme difficulty working out that words are made of different sounds and that there is a pattern to language. Although they suffer no physical difficulty or hearing loss, they just cannot make out the differences between sounds, or make sounds in a sequence.

Children with these types of difficulties benefit from receiving specialist support as soon as possible.

Stammering (also known as *stuttering)*

This is a difficulty with talking fluently. Children who stammer find it hard to talk without lots of stops and starts, or repeating the same sound or word over and over again.

Most young children between two and a half and four years of age go through a period on *non-fluency.*

This does not necessarily mean that they will be stammer in adult life. However, it is very important that we are aware of how we respond to children in this phase. It is particularly helpful to listen carefully to what the children are saying, and to give them plenty of time before you respond.

'Things I like' boxes

This activity helps
Understanding between children and adults, leading to improved well-being, relaxation, listening, and enjoyment of talking!

Resources needed:
A shoebox
Coloured wrapping paper and small items to decorate the box
Objects / toys from home

Activity:
With the child, cover the shoe box in wrapping paper, and decorate it with things such as photos of the child, glitter, drawings and stickers. Ask parents to put in the box a few objects or toys from home that the child will like and will want to talk about.

To introduce the idea, decorate your own 'Things I like box' and fill it with objects and photos of objects you like. You might want to put in a few objects you are confident the children will like; e.g. a soft toy from a children's TV programme or film, or photos of you with the children. Show these to the children and parents to encourage them to make one together at home.

You can use the boxes in all sorts of different ways: as something to chat about individually or in a group and they can be a focal point to help children who are finding it difficult to settle. The boxes generate a huge amount of interest, stimulate language development, and can be an important part of the process of helping children to settle into your setting.

Important points:
- Avoid making this a 'show and tell' activity to the whole group. These boxes are best shared individually, in pairs, or in small groups.
- Send the boxes home regularly so parents and children can talk about what they want to put in next.

'All about me' boxes

This activity helps
Understanding between children and adults, leading to improved wellbeing, relaxation, listening, and enjoyment of talking!

Resources needed:
A cardboard shoebox
Coloured wrapping paper and small items to decorate the box
Objects and photos from home

Activity:
An 'all about me' box is a decorated shoebox containing objects and photos that help us share conversations with children about their lives at home.

Ask parents to decorate a cardboard shoebox. The box could be covered in wrapping paper decorated with photos of the child and their name. Inside the box they can put photographs of the child when they were a baby, playing with favourite toys, important relatives, the front of their house, and their family car and pets.

Encourage parents to involve the child in decorating the box at home and choosing with their family what photos and objects can go inside. It is important to talk about the completed box with the child and his parents, so that everyone is aware what is inside and what the photos mean. For example, the names of relatives and what the children call them (children often have special names for their grandparents).
The box should be kept in a safe place and brought out to share with children at quiet times. They can also be shared with small groups of children.

'All about me' boxes can often become very special objects for the children and family, so they must to be treated with care and respect. Conversations with the children about the contents of the boxes often help children to feel reassured if they are unhappy about separating from their parents. They are also particularly useful in helping us understand what children with speech and language difficulties are saying, which adds to wellbeing and helps their confidence as talkers.

Chatterboxes

A chatterbox is a box containing toys and objects based on a theme or story. Children take the boxes home and explore the contents with their parents.

This activity helps:
To create understanding between children and adults, leading to improved wellbeing, relaxation, listening, and enjoyment of talking; vocabulary development and interest in books.

Resources needed:
A strong plastic storage box with a lid, that must be no smaller than a shoe box.
Toys, objects, fiction and non-fiction books all related to a theme
Notebook and pen
Laminated inventory
Suggestion cards

Activity:
Choose a topic that you know your children are interested in, or that you know will spark their excitement, e.g. diggers, aliens, farm animals, football, bath time, birthdays, birds, or a favourite story. Collect toys and objects that are related to the topic. For example, a 'bird watching' chatterbox could contain a soft toy bird, a simple information book about birds, a pair of toy binoculars and a recipe for 'bird cake' (food for our feathered friends, not a cake containing garden birds!), and a story book like *'Owl babies'*.

Include simple guidelines on how to use the box, i.e.

- Only to be used when the parent has enough time to give the child full attention.
- The box should be put away when not in use, and items should not be left lying around.

It is useful to include a simple 'prompt card' with ideas for the type of questions parents might like to ask, or how to develop the child's interest further. Parents can use the notebook and pen to comment on how the child responds to the Chatterbox.
Chatterboxes were designed by Tracey Spence, Advisory teacher for children with speech and language difficulties, Luton. For more information contact tracey.spence@luton.gov.uk

What's happening next?

A regular routine helps children feel secure, and promotes understanding and language development. Children with speech and language difficulties often need support to understand and learn their routine. They may have difficulties with finishing one activity and moving onto another, and often need to be told individually about a change, because they find it difficult to tune into a group instruction.

This activity helps:

A sense of wellbeing; understanding of language; vocabulary development

Resources needed:

Songs to sing about routine events
Music to signal a change

Clear language

Give the children plenty of notice that you are changing activities. Use clear instructions, e.g. "It's time to go inside now." rather than, "Shall we go in now?" or "We are all getting ready for story now," rather than, "I'm sorry but we have to stop now. Shall we get ready for a story? Is that OK?"

It can be helpful to check that children have understood and to help them practice the language of routines by encouraging them to fill in the last part of your sentence, e.g. "We are putting on our coats because it's time to… (go home!)"

Clear signals

Use a piece of music or a musical instrument as a signal that it is time to change activities. Sing a song for each key activity and time of the day: tidying up, washing hands, sitting in a circle, welcoming everyone, going to sleep, singing goodbye and going home. This gives the children a clear signal and helps them understand what they should be doing.

Visual clues and timetables

Children need visual clues to help them understand what is happening now, and what they will be expected to do next.

Resources needed:
Objects linked to key events in the children's day
Photographs of key events in the children's day

Visual clues for routine events
Before you tell children about snack time or that the 'rolling snack bar' will open, cover a table with a plastic tablecloth that has fruit or food designs on it.
Just before you tell everyone it's time to go outside, put on your coat and pick up a child's coat.
Prior to getting into groups, show the children photographs of group time and objects from the activity in which they will be taking part.

Visual timetables
This is a display of a series of photos showing the main events in the children's day. These work best if the photos include children doing the activities, and if they are displayed at the children's eye level. Laminate the photos and back them with Velcro. Talk to the children at the beginning of the session, and help them to stick the photos on the wall in the order that they happen. Ask the children to help you to remove a photo when each activity has finished.
Some children are helped by a 'now and next' board. Put a board on the wall with the words 'now' and 'next' on it. Under 'now' have a photo of what you are already doing, and under 'next' a photo of what is going to happen. Talk to the children about the photos, and involve them in helping you change them once an activity has finished.

Having photos on a small key ring attached to your clothes helps you talk to the children about changes from one activity to another while you are on the move, e.g. outside or on a trip.

What's hiding?

This activity helps:
Taking turns; children looking at and responding to each other; learning each other's names; understanding of language; expressive language; vocabulary development.

Resources needed:
A blanket or large cloth.
A soft toy that makes a noise when you squeeze it or press a button.
A bag of large soft toys, e.g. farm animals

Simple activity (with two children)
Let the children play with the noisy toy. After a short while, ask them to stop playing and close their eyes. Hide a toy under the blanket and then squeeze or press it to make the noise. Can the children guess what is under the blanket? Were they correct?
Bring four of the soft toys out of the bag. Let the children handle the toys and help them to name them. Hide these toys under the blanket and ask the children to take turns to put their hand under the blanket to find a toy. Before they take it out, can they guess what it is? Were they right?

Harder activity
Repeat this activity, but in a group.
If the children are not happy with the toy they have found, they can then swap it with someone else!

Extension activity
Leave a small part of the cuddly toy sticking out from under the cloth. Can they guess what it is? How did they know?

Who's hiding?

This activity helps:
Taking turns; children looking at and responding to each other; learning each other's names; understanding of language.

Resources needed:
A blanket or large cloth.

Simple activity with three children
Explain to the children that you are going to play a hiding game. When they close their eyes, you will tap someone on the hand, and that person will hide under the blanket. Can they guess who is hiding?

Harder activity
Try this with a larger group.

Extension activities
- When the child is hiding, uncover a small part of them from under the blanket (foot, hand, pony tail etc.) Ask questions like, "Is this a boy or a girl? How do you know? Where were they sitting?"
- You can play the same game, but instead of hiding under a blanket, ask the child to go outside the door with an adult.

Important point
Some children will be worried at the thought of going under the blanket. Respect this, and choose children first who seem very keen. Reluctant children often join in if you play this game regularly.

Photo card games

This activity helps:
Taking turns; children looking at and responding to each other; learning each other's names; understanding of language.

Resources needed:
A *photo card* for each child in the group.

A photo card is a large photo (A5 size is ideal) of a child's or adult's head and shoulders, stuck onto a piece of coloured card. Ideally, the card should be laminated or covered in clear sticky back plastic, as it will be handled a lot.
Beneath the child's photo attach the child's name. The name should be printed from a computer, laminated and backed with *Velcro*. This can be later used in name recognition games. Some settings use the children's photo cards for registration, 'welcome time', and circle games to help develop face recognition and the learning of names.

Simple activity with two or three children
Use photocards, facing down, of the adults and the children taking part in this game. Each of you will take it in turns to pick up a card, say the name of the person on the photo, and give them their card.

Harder activity
Repeat this game with a larger group.

Extension activities

- Before you start, ask each child in the group to choose two photocards of children in the setting whose names they know. Hide all the photo cards under a blanket. Take turns to find a card. Can they say the children's names?
- Place all the photocards face up on the floor, with each one half covered by a piece of paper. Ask each child to guess who it is. Is he/she a boy or a girl?
- Repeat these activities regularly so that, eventually, you are able to include the photocards of lots of children in your setting, and not just those in a small group. Can children sort them into 'boys and girls', 'my best friend', 'who I like playing with' etc?

More photo card games

This activity helps:
Taking turns; children looking at and responding to each other; learning each other's names; understanding of language.

Resources needed:
A set of children's and adults' photo cards; one for each person in the group.
A box of interesting toys
A set of small wooden bricks
A small bag containing objects and pictures representing the children's favourite songs

Game 1 Choose a toy
Children and adults sit in a circle, with the photocards spread out in the middle of the circle, facing down. Each child takes a turn to pick up a card, name the child in the photo, and pass him his card. The child on the photo gets to choose a toy from the box. Keep going until all the children have received their photocard and chosen a toy. Don't like the toy you have chosen? Then swap!

Game 2 Build a tower
As above, but each child chooses a brick to build a tower. Try again with two bricks each, then three!

Game 3 Sing a song
As above, but use a bag of objects and pictures representing the children's favourite songs. As a child's photocard is picked up they choose an object from the bag, and you all sing the song.

Whose car?

This activity helps:
Taking turns; children looking at and responding to each other; learning each other's names; understanding of language; expressive language; vocabulary development.

Resources needed:
A box containing different coloured cars
A blanket or large cloth.

Simple activity
Each child takes a turn to choose a car. Encourage each child to look closely at their car and talk about what it looks like – the shape, the colour, the size etc. When the children are ready, place all the cars under the blanket. Children take turns to find a car, and say who it belonged to.

Harder activity
Repeat this activity in this session, or in later sessions, using fruit, dinosaurs, a train and carriages, coloured bricks, TV-related toys etc.

Extension activities
- Try adding books to each activity; e.g. if you are choosing dinosaurs, have a dinosaur book for each toy. Hide the books as well as the toys.
- Whose shoes? Ask each child and adult to take off one shoe. Put them under the blanket. Take turns to find a shoe and match it with its owner.
- Whose socks? As for 'whose shoes' but with your socks!

Pass along!

This activity helps:
Taking turns; vocabulary (especially names); listening

Resources needed:
The children's own coats, bags or boots (they need to be labelled).
A large pillow case or bag

Simple activity
Put the objects in the bag. Take it in turns to open the bag and pull out the object. Find out who it belongs to; then pass it to them. This game is great when played with just a few children; when they are changing to go outside.

Harder activity
Place items of the children's clothing on the floor in front of you. Take turns to choose one item and put it into the bag. Each child tries to remember what is in the bag and who it belongs to. Increase this to two items each.

Extension activity
Whoever has the bag looks inside and has to describe the object before they take it out; For example, the child would say, "It's a red lunchbox", before passing it along to the person it belongs to.

Find the penguin

This activity helps:
Vocabulary development; taking turns; understanding questions

Resources needed:
An animal picture / photo book with a penguin in it.
A bag of small cuddly toys, including a toy penguin. Each toy should match an animal from the book.
A large cloth.

Simple activity with one child
Share the book with the child, asking, "Is that a penguin?", as you turn each page. This will encourage him to tell you what you are pointing at. Take the toys from the bag, one at a time, asking, "Is that a penguin?" Match the toys to the pictures.

Harder activity
Repeat the activity with a small group of children.

Extension activity
Put the cloth in the middle of the circle. Ask the children to shut their eyes. Put all the toys under the cloth.
Take turns to take out a toy from under the cloth. Ask each child, "Is that a penguin?"
You will find that they will enjoy saying, "No!" and telling you what the object is. If they don't know, then you can tell them! Give a big cheer when someone pulls out the penguin. Then start again, looking for the penguin, or choosing another animal to look for.

You don't have to use penguins; it could be any animal, or object that you know children can name and are interested in.

Swapsies

This activity helps:
Taking turns; children looking at and responding to each other; learning each other's names; understanding of language; expressive language; vocabulary development.

Resources needed:
A collection of soft toy animals, or small soft toys linked to children's TV programmes and films
A large cloth bag

Simple activity: played with you and one child.
Take out two toys from the bag. Give one to the child and keep one for yourself. (It helps if you choose for yourself the toy that you know he will want). Ask him if he would like to swap. Bring out more toys, one at a time, and encourage swapping.

Harder activity
Played with two children

Extension activity: played in a group
Children and adults sit in a circle. Hand out the soft toys at random around the group, so that each child and adult has one each.
Ask the children to say what they have (or tell them if they don't know what it is called).
Help the children to swap with each other, until everyone is happy with what they have got.

Important note
Swapping is not easy! Be prepared to support children in this activity, and the more you repeat it, the easier it gets.

Wrap it up!

This activity helps:
Taking turns; children looking at and responding to each other; learning each other's names; understanding of language; expressive language; vocabulary development.

Resources needed:
At least two rolls of wrapping paper, featuring different designs.
A roll of masking tape
A collection of small soft toys (Characters from television and films are particularly popular. For example: Bob the Builder, In the Night Garden, Thomas the Tank Engine etc.)

Simple activity, with three children
Give each child a toy. Not happy with it? Then swap!
Help the children to choose some wrapping paper, and to wrap up their toy.
When everyone has wrapped their toy, play 'pass the parcel'.

Harder activities
- Give the children two toys each, and have three colours of wrapping paper.
- Play the game again, but with only one colour of paper.

Extension activity
Play the game in a big group.

Busy bodies

This activity helps:
Vocabulary development, particularly action words

Resources needed:
Laminated photographs of children from your setting
Velcro
A board with a felt surface, or any surface to which Velcro will attach.

Simple activity
Take photos of the children doing different actions (running, jumping, sleeping, cooking etc.)
Copy and laminate two sets. Can the children match the pictures and name the action?

Harder activity
Take photos of children in your setting, standing up straight with their legs apart, and arms stretching out sideways. Cut each of the photos down the middle. Laminate each half, and stick Velcro on the back of each half. Can the children match up the different halves: firstly on a table, and then by sticking them on the board?
This activity can be done individually, then in pairs, working up to larger groups.

Make more copies of the photos, but this time cut off the children's arms, legs and heads. Laminate these and play with them, as above.

Extension activities
- Take photos of the children playing with different toys in different parts of the nursery. Can the children tell you who is in the photo, and what they are doing?
- Copy these photos again and cut them in half. Can the children match up the halves?

Clothes shop

This activity helps:
Vocabulary development

Resources needed:
Children's clothes. (This activity can be made very exciting by collecting clothes that might be worn by slightly older children, such as school uniform, football kit, wet weather clothes etc.)

Simple activity
Set up a role play clothes shop. Encourage the children to try on the clothes and name them.

Harder activity
Help the children to sort out the clothes into different categories: boys / girls; hot / cold / rainy weather; baby clothes / big children's clothes etc.

Extension activities

- Take photos of the children dressed up in the clothes. Make a display with the children with the clothes pinned to the wall and labelled clearly.
- Cut out pictures from clothes catalogues. Sort them into categories and stick them onto different pieces of paper, or make a collage for the display.

How do I put it on?

This activity helps:
Vocabulary of clothing, parts of the body, and actions

Resources needed:
Two large teddies or puppets ('boy' and 'girl'), big enough for children's clothes to fit on them.
Real children's clothes that fit the teddy / puppet
A blanket

Simple activity, with one or two children
Begin with one puppet / teddy and a set of clothes. Teddy doesn't know how to get dressed. What does he put on first? His pants? Where does he put them? On his head? How does he put them on? Can we help him to get dressed?

Harder activity, with a group of children
Spread the blanket in the middle of the group. Hide the clothes underneath. Each child takes turns to take out an item of clothing. What is it? What do we put on teddy first? Take turns to put the clothes on teddy, in the right order.

Extension activity
Introduce the 'girl' puppet, and repeat, as above. Do the children make a distinction between what the girl might wear (especially knickers v pants!). For some children colour of clothes is very important, i.e. pink for girls and blue for boys. This is not necessarily a good thing, but if children do have very strong ideas about what boys and girls should wear, then this can be something very useful to talk about.

"I like / don't like"

This activity helps:

Just like adults, children love to talk about what they like and don't like to eat. If we know what children don't like, then we can begin to ask them questions like "Why not?" These are important early steps in developing conversations with children. Start by talking with the children at meal and snack times, and then introducing games.

Resources needed:

Food items we know children like and can't stand!
A teddy or puppet
A bag

Simple activities

At snack time, put out food items that you know the child really likes and those that he doesn't. Talk about what you like and dislike, and why. Encourage the children to say what they like / dislike.

Harder activity

In a group, take food items out of the bag, one at a time. Ask the children to sort out what they like and don't like.
Tell the children if you like the food or not, and why not.
(Start with real items, then toys, and finally picture books)

Extension activities

Feed teddy various foods. Does teddy like them or not? Begin by using real food. Later on play the same game with toy food, and finally with pictures.

What's in the box?

This activity helps:
Naming and describing objects.

Resources needed:
A shoe box with a lid
A collection of toys, small enough to put inside the shoe box.

Simple activity
Start with five toys that the children can definitely name. Place them in front of the children. Ask them to close their eyes, and then put an object in the box. Can they guess what you have taken away and put in the box? If not, give a verbal clue, e.g. 'You eat it / you put it on your head / you drive it'. Still stuck? Then say the first part of the word; "You drive it, and it's a c…" If they are really stuck try giving a visual clue, e.g. remove the lid slightly and allow the children to take a quick peek at part of the object.

Harder activity
Children take turns to hide an object while you close your eyes.
You can make this game more challenging by increasing the number of objects to choose from, or putting more than one object in the box.

Extension activities
- Don't show the children the objects before you put them in the box. Describe to the children what is inside the box, including what you do with it, its colour, and its shape. Can they tell you what is inside before they take it out?
- Use objects from different categories, e.g. from the bathroom, toys, clothes, footwear.

What's in the feely box?

This activity helps:
Naming and describing objects.

Resources needed:
A 'feely box' (a sealed cardboard box with a hole in the side, that children and adults can reach inside.)
A collection of toys and objects: small enough to put inside the feely box.

Simple activity
Start with five toys that the children can definitely name. Place them in front of the children. Ask them to close their eyes, and put an object in the box. Take turns to feel inside the box. Can they guess what is inside?

Harder activity
- Use objects that the children have not seen.
- Children take turns to hide an object while you close your eyes.
- You can make this game more challenging by increasing the number of objects to choose from, or putting more than one object in the feely box.

Extension activities
- Help the children to describe what is in the box, before they name it; e.g. "It is soft and round. I think it is a ball."
- Help each child to put an object in the box while the others are not looking.

Who's in the box?

This activity helps:
Social development; learning each other's names

Resources needed:
A cardboard box, large enough for a child to hide inside
A shoe box
Photos of the children
A collection of small toys

Simple activity
Use the box that is big enough for a child to climb into. Everyone should close their eyes. Choose someone to hide. Who is hiding? Call their name. Were you right?

Harder activity
Use the shoebox and photographs. Spread out the photographs in front of the children.
The children close their eyes while you put a photo in the box. Who is hiding?
Were they correct?
When everyone has had a go, repeat the game but this time you put in two photos at a time.
Repeat again with the children taking turns to put the photos in the box while everyone else closes their eyes.

Extension activities
- Use the big box. Put out the toys in front of the children. When everyone has their eyes closed, choose a child and a toy to hide in the box. Can the children guess who is in there, and what they have taken?
- Repeat this activity but use the shoebox, photos of the children, and photos of objects.

Socks!

This activity helps:
Conversation; vocabulary; sorting; matching, and the concept of *'the same'*.

Resources needed:
Pairs of socks
Teddy bear
A collection of soft toys

Simple activity
Ask children to help you sort out your pile of socks. As they do it, talk about the colours and patterns. Can they *match* them up? Which ones are the *same*? Put pairs of socks on the teddy bear.

Harder activity
Introduce a collection of soft toys. Play with them with the children, and then help them to stuff them inside some socks. Can they remember which toy was in which sock? Ask the children to close their eyes while you hide a toy inside a sock. When the children open their eyes, show them the sock and see if they can guess what is inside. It can be great fun to leave a little bit of the toy showing to help them guess what it is.

Extension activities

- Once you have stuffed the toys into the socks, play 'pass the sock'. (It's the same as 'pass the parcel' but with socks instead!)
- Introduce different types of socks, e.g. football socks, trainer socks and tights. What are they called, and who might wear them?

Socks on the line

This activity helps:
Conversation; vocabulary; sorting; matching, and the concept of *'the same'*.

Resources needed:
Pairs of socks
String
Clothes pegs
Soft toys

Simple activity
Rig up a simple 'washing line'. Peg onto the line one sock from each pair. Give the children a sock each and see if they can find one on the line that is the same.

Harder activity
Hang some socks on the line, with a soft toy inside each sock. (Use as many socks as there are children in the group.) Give each child a sock that matches one on the line. Ask each child to find their matching sock on the line, and find out what is inside.

Extension activity
Give the children two pieces of white card each in the shape of a sock. Help them to colour in their socks the same colour. Play the same game as the simple activity above, but using the cardboard socks.

Tidy up time

This activity helps:
Conversation; vocabulary; sorting; matching, and the concept of *'the same'*.

Resources needed:
Clearly labelled containers for resources (ideally with a photo of the resource, its name and a piece of the resource stuck on the front of the container.)

Simple activity
Help children put away one collection / group of toys at a time, e.g. a train set or the books.
Name the parts of the train set as you put them away.

Harder activity
Help children sort out two sets of toys into appropriate containers, e.g. cars and the train set.
Ask children to pass to you cars of different colours and sizes.

Extension activity
Gradually increase the number of sets of toys.
Encourage the children to talk about where things go and help them describe what they are, e.g. size and colour.

Lids!

This activity helps:
Conversation; vocabulary; sorting, matching; the concept of *'the same'*.

Resources needed:
A large collection of metal lids from jars; e.g. jam, pasta sauce, drinks, baby food, pickles.
Containers of various shapes and sizes, e.g. metal biscuit tins, plastic ice cream tubs, cake tins.
Coloured rugs to sit on

Simple activity
Sit on the rugs with the children and play together with the collection of lids and containers. Comment on what they do and say.

Harder activity
Encourage the children to sort the lids by colour. (This works particularly well when you are tidying them all away!)

Extension activity
Encourage the children to help each other to fill up all the containers. Talk about the different types of lids; colour, size, what sort of jar they might have come from, their favourite lids etc.
Some lids make a noise when they click them. Can they find all the lids that click?

Tip
If you ask parents, local hotels, cafes and care homes to collect lids for you, you will acquire a huge collection in no time!

Things that go together

This activity helps:
Conversation; vocabulary; sorting; matching

Resources needed:
Everyday objects from around the settings and home that children will recognise as going together, e.g. cup and saucer, bowl and spoon, soap and towel, toothbrush and toothpaste, shoes and socks.
A big cloth bag

Simple activity
Help the child to match the objects and talk about what they are used for, and why they go together.

Harder activity
In a small group, put all the objects in a big bag. Pass the bag around, and ask each child to take out an object. When two objects go together, ask the two children to sit together or swap what they have got.

Extension activity
Help the children to match the objects and then group them into various rooms that they might come from, e.g. bathroom, kitchen, bedroom, outside. Can they tell you where they come from and why they go together?

Boy or girl?

This activity helps:
Conversation; vocabulary; sorting; matching; learning each other's names

Resources needed:
Photo cards of children in the setting, or photos of each child
Items of clothing belonging to children in the setting; e.g. coats or hats (all clearly labelled)
Magazines with pictures of children; e.g. from toy catalogues

Simple activity
With one child, ask them to sort the photos into boys and girls.

Harder activity
Repeat the 'simple' activity with a pair of children: ideally a boy and a girl. Start by getting the girl to collect all of the girl photos and the boy to collecting all of the photos of boys.

Repeat the activity in reverse with the girl collecting the boy photos and the boy collecting the girl photos.

Collect children's clothing items from their pegs (e.g. hats and coats). Can the children sort the clothes into those that belong to boys or girls? You might need to go round the setting asking all the children so you can find out! (This activity can be done before everyone goes out to play or at home time.)

Extension activity
- Using the magazines, cut out pictures of girls and boys, and talk about what they are doing and wearing.
- Share non-fiction books together. Talk about how objects, animals and people can be grouped together. For example, horses, dogs and cats are *animals*; bears, tigers, and lions are *wild animals*; chairs, sofas, tables, and beds are all *furniture*; houses, bungalows, caravans, and flats are all *places where people live*; Father Christmas, Postman Pat, Bob the Builder, and Fireman Sam are all *men.*

What is it like?

These activities can take place naturally, e.g. as part of preparing for snack time and cooking, as activities with individual children, or in a group.

This activity helps:
Vocabulary development, expressive language, sorting

Resources needed:
Food items, e.g. fruit, vegetables, breakfast cereals, baby food, crisps, biscuits, different types of bread, drinks, and soups.

Simple activity
Use food items with which the children are familiar.
Prepare the foods together and sort into foods they like or dislike.

Harder activity
Introduce unfamiliar foods, e.g. coconuts, porridge, various pastes for spreading on toast.
Help the children to describe what the foods feel, sound, smell and taste like.
Help them to explain why they don't like something, using words like *yucky, horrible, nasty, disgusting* etc.

Extension activity
Sort foods into different categories: fruit, vegetables, cereals, baby food, and for different meals.
Use toy food in the role play area and introduce the same activities and language as part of children's play.

Rhyme and song bags

This activity helps:
Development of speech sounds; phonological awareness.

Resources needed:
A cloth bag.
Toys that represent a song or rhyme, e.g. a star for 'Twinkle twinkle', a spider for 'Incey, wincey spider.'
Pictures (on card and laminated) that illustrate the songs and rhymes.
Rhymes and songs on CD or MP3 player.

Simple activity
With one or two children, take out one object at a time, talk about what song it represents and sing the song together.

Harder activity
A group of children take turns to take out an object and sing the song.
(What makes this activity hard for children is having to take turns and accepting that they may not get the object they wanted. If they are really not happy, then let them swap with someone else!)

Extension activity
Place the toys on the floor. Hum the first few lines of a song, or play the introduction.
Can the children choose the right toy before they hear the words of the song?
Repeat the activity with pictures.
Encourage the children to learn the words to as many songs or rhymes as possible.

Our favourite song

This activity helps:
Phonological awareness; speech development; mathematical thinking

Resources needed:
A decorated shoebox with a slot in the lid
Pieces of paper to write on
A small bag with puppets / pictures / objects representing six nursery rhymes.

The activity:
Show the toys to each child in the setting and ask them to choose the toy that corresponds to their favourite rhyme or song.
Together write on the paper both their name and the name of the rhyme. Then draw a picture of the object
Help the child to fold the paper and put it through the slot into the box.

This can be a very absorbing process so be prepared to allow at least five minutes per child!

When all the children have taken part, put the objects / puppets in a row in the middle of the circle. One-by-one, take out the children's pieces of paper and place them in a row under each object. Soon you will have a simple block graph and children can see the 'results' emerging. At regular intervals, ask the children "Which song has the most pieces of paper? How many has 'Twinkle, twinkle' got? Who do you think is going to be the winner?" etc. When all the pieces of paper have been laid out, announce the winner, and sing the song together.

Extension activities
Involve parents by asking them what songs they sang together when they were young. This can lead to a display. Invite parents and grandparents to share songs with the children.
Organise a nursery rhyme day for all the family with craft and play activities.

Ready, steady, go!

This activity helps:
Listening games are vital for very young children to tune them into what we have to say and to learn about taking turns (which is a vital skill for having conversations).

Resources needed:
Play outdoors; on a swing, or down a slide.
A set of small toy cars, wooden bricks or stones.
A length of plastic guttering and downpipe.

Simple activity
Push the child on the swing. Every time the swing comes back to you, hold onto it. Say, "Ready, steady…", and only let go when the child says, "Go!"
The child sits at the bottom of the slide. You have a collection of toy cars. Say, "Ready, steady…" and release them when the child says, "Go!"
Swap places so the child is at the top of the slide, and get him to release the cars when you say, "Go!"

Harder activity
Repeat the same activities with two children until they are able to give each other instructions and can play together while you watch.

Extension activity
Tilt the guttering at an angle and encourage the children to shoot down cars, wooden bricks and small stones after the signal of "Ready, steady, go!" Use the downpipe and encourage a group of children to play the same game.

Listening walk

This activity helps:
Listening; concentration; vocabulary; expressive language

Resources needed:
Photographs of sources of sounds you are likely to hear in your outdoor area (including the street).
Two sets of identical musical instruments

Simple activity
Go for a walk in your outdoor area. What sounds can we hear? Cars? A lorry? A police car? Birds? An aeroplane?
Go back indoors and show the child the photos. Ask them to choose one. Go outside again and listen for the sound they chose.

Harder activity
Repeat the activity with a group of children.

Extension activity
Using the sets of musical instruments put one set at various points in your outdoor area.
With a group of children, show them the matching set and ask each child to choose one to play. Can they find the same one outside?
Play an instrument and see if they can go outside and find the same one.
Hide your instruments behind a screen. Play one and send the children outside to find it.
Repeat the activity, but with children choosing which instruments to play.

Musical chairs

This activity helps:
Listening; Awareness of other children

Resources needed:
CD player
Lively music
Some chairs

Simple activity
Play with two children and six chairs in a line.
When the music starts, the children run or dance carefully around the chairs. When the music stops, both children sit down on the chair nearest to them. Take away one chair each time until there is only one chair left. The 'winner' is the child who sits down first on the last chair. (It is better to do it this way so the children have practice and don't get too upset if they lose)

Harder activity
Repeat this with a small group of children, with more chairs than children.

Extension activity
Repeat this activity with a small group, but with one chair for each child.

Pass the parcel

This activity helps:
Pass the parcel can be played with just about any objects, and is a great way of developing vocabulary.

Resources needed:
Wrapping paper of different colours.
Small plastic animals.
Masking tape.
Music on CD

Simple activity
In a small group, ask the children to choose an animal. Help each child to wrap theirs in a small amount of wrapping paper and to stick it with masking tape.
Collect up the 'parcels'. When the music starts, pass around the parcels one at a time. When the music stops, whoever has the parcel gets to open it up. Before they do, can anyone remember whose parcel it is?

Harder activity
Repeat the activity, but with wrapping paper of only one colour.

Extension activity
Use two sets of identical animals, or a set of adult and baby animals.
As the parcels are unwrapped, can they match the animals?
Use sets of musical instruments, instead of toys. Can they guess what is inside as it is being passed around?
Use objects that represent favourite nursery rhymes and songs. The 'winner' of each round gets to sing the song.

Let's pretend

This activity helps:
Role play and imaginative play don't always come naturally to children with speech and language difficulties. Start role playing by using real objects in a real way and gradually introducing imaginative props. As an example, we might feed teddy with real biscuits before we use toy biscuits. It helps to share real experiences together and then role play about them, e.g. filling up a real washing machine and hanging out the washing and then pretending to do this in the role play area.
These activities introduce children to the world of pretending, which develops their imaginations and use of imaginative language.

Resources needed:
A big cardboard box, big enough for children to sit inside
Red paint and brushes
A steering wheel
A chair

Simple activity
Ideally, go on an outing on a bus. Talk about buses and sing 'The wheels on the bus'.
Paint the box together and turn it into a 'bus' by adding windows, wheels and even windscreen wipers. Cut down one side of the bus at the 'back'.
Put the chair inside, so that the children can take turns to be the driver, using the steering wheel to drive, while everyone sings 'The wheels on the bus'.

Harder activity
Repeat the activity until children are able to play together with adults supporting.

Extension activity
Help children to use small chairs to pretend that they are on a bus, in a car, or on a train.
Add dressing up clothes and even tools; the bus might break down and a policeman and mechanic might come along to fix it!

Small world play

This activity helps:
Play with small animals, people and transport is an extension of role play and is very important for developing both imagination and imaginative language.

Resources needed:
Soft toy or puppet farm animals
Small plastic animals
Play dough
Thick felt pens
Sheets of large white paper (Lining paper from hardware shops is ideal)
Masking tape
Story books and non-fiction books about farm animals
A small group of children

Simple activity
Cover two small tables with lining paper, fasten down with masking tape.
Sit on the floor with the children. Share out the soft toys. Alternatively, you can hide them under a blanket, and children can take turns to take an animal out. Help the children to name the animals and practice making animal noises. Pass round the non-fiction books, and talk together about animals, what they eat where they live etc.
Move to the table. Introduce the small animals and felt pens. Can the children draw some grass for the cows and horses to eat?
Can they make a pond and river for the ducks and geese? What about drawing some mud for the pigs?
Introduce play dough, and the children can make houses, fences, trees, and anything that captures their imaginations.

Extension activities
As the children are busy at the table, show them pictures from a story book about farm animals.
End the session with the story and sing 'Old MacDonald had a farm.'

Telling stories

This activity helps:
It is very important that children can talk about something that *has happened*, and especially to someone who wasn't there.
The activity below boosts children's confidence, and is particularly helpful for children with speech difficulties who may have plenty to say but are difficult to understand.

Resources needed:
An exciting activity
A digital camera
Some stickers
A parent or relative

Simple activity
Share an exciting activity, e.g. going down the slide, blowing bubbles, playing with a new toy.
Talk with the child as you play and take photographs. When you have finished, tell the child that, " It will be great to tell Mummy all about what we have been doing when she comes to collect you."
Throughout the session, and with the child present, show the photos to other children and staff, and practice telling everyone what you have been doing. When the parent or carer comes to collect their child, show them the objects and the photos, and help the child to talk simply about what you did together.

Harder activity
Take photos and make a small book that the child can look at every day. Add to it as often as you can so the child has lots of activities to talk about with their friends and family.

Extension activity
When you have done something new together, give the child a sticker to wear.
When the parent or carer comes to collect the child, help the child to explain why they have been given the sticker.

Sharing books

This activity helps:

Many children with speech and language difficulties need help to enjoy books. They may prefer non-fiction books with photos, as these are easier to interpret than stories.
Sharing a book works best when the child chooses the book, and is encouraged to hold it themselves. This means that they can turn the pages when they want to and they will be more likely to feel that they are in charge of what is talked about. This is particularly important for children who need to practice talking!

Resources needed:

Fiction and non-fiction books
Toys and objects linked to the books.
A cloth bag

Simple activity

Find out what the child's interests are, e.g. cars, diggers, animals, princesses, TV programmes.
Choose a subject and fill a cloth bag with toys and a non-fiction book linked to the subject.
Play with the toys and share the book together.

Harder activity

Repeat the activity, but with two children.

Extension activity

Introduce a fiction book related to the children's particular interests.
Cut up magazines together, linked to the children's special interest. Make a collage and display it in the book area.
Repeat the 'simple' activity but with a story book.

Enjoying storytime

This activity helps:
Many children need support to make the most of sharing a story in a group. Sharing games and activities linked to the story boosts their vocabulary and knowledge of the story, which helps them to join in when the book is shared in a group.

Resources needed:
A story book
A related non-fiction book
Activities and games linked to the books

Activity in a small group
Choose a non-fiction book to share which features a subject of interest to the children, for example, cars.
Play games with the cars (see 'Small world play' and 'Let's pretend' for ideas.) Draw a road on the large sheet of paper and, together, 'drive' the cars along it. As you are talking and playing, introduce the non-fiction book and then the story, showing the children the main pictures.
Sing a linked song as you play.

When they are ready, share the story with the small group of children.
At the end of the session, share the toys and books with a large group and encourage the children from the small group to share what they know before you tell the story.
Sing your linked song at the end.

Make up a story outdoors

This activity helps:
Vocabulary; expressive language; imaginative language

Resources needed:
Animal puppets
Fruit

Simple activity
Hide the animal puppets around the outdoor area. With a small group of children, 'find' the puppets one at a time. As you go along, make up a very simple story about the children and the animals, e.g. Jamie went for a walk and he found a monkey, and the monkey said, "Ooh, Ooh, Ooh!" Then Jasmine met a lion and it roared at her.

Harder activity
As you find the animals, make up a more complex story, involving an animal as the character, e.g. A monkey was lost and he wanted his mum. He met a lion who said, "I'll help you to find her." Then they met a giraffe who said, "Let's find something to eat." They found a banana, and then they found mum and everyone was happy.

Extension activity
Involve a group of children in acting out a simple story that they already know. *Handa's surprise* by Eileen Browne or *Going on a bear hunt* by Michael Rosen and Helen Oxenbury are good starting points.

Comics

This activity helps:
Sharing comics with children can help develop their spoken language as well as lead even very young children into a love of books. Many comics are based on popular children's TV and film characters, so provide a natural focus for chat and creativity!

Resources needed:
Children's comics (laminating the pages makes them last longer) or comic annuals
Children's TV and film toys and soft toy characters
Books based on TV programmes and films
Theme tunes from children's TV programmes and films.

Activity
Play with the TV toys, and share the comics together. Play the theme tunes and sing the songs together.
Children find this activity hugely enjoyable, and especially if you can let them choose their favourite characters to play with, talk about and read about.

Harder activity
Cut out pictures of characters from different comics and stick them onto pieces of card.. Can the children sort them out and name them? Give them one card each. Can they find a book or comic that has the same character?

Extension activity
Cover a table with lining paper. Encourage children to draw their favourite characters from the comics and books.

USEFUL WEBSITES

General ideas for singing, stories, and language development:

www.talk4meaning.co.uk	Michael Jones' website
www.bbc.co.uk/cbeebies	Fun and games related to the BBC TV channel for young children
www.bookstart.org.uk	An organisation promoting books and language development
www.literacytrust.org.uk/early_years	Promoting early reading and talking

Stages of speech and language development:

www.talktoyourbaby.org.uk	Promoting young children's wellbeing and early communication.
www.talkingpoint.org.uk	Providing information on children's communication

If you are concerned and want specific advice:

www.talk4meaning.co.uk	Michael Jones's website
www.ican.org.uk	ICAN is a major charity supporting children's communication
www.rcslt.org.uk	Royal College of Speech and Language Therapists
www.afasic.org.uk	AFASIC: a charity supporting children with specific speech and language difficulties
www.nhs.uk/choices	Provides information on medical issues, e.g. hearing problems.
www.dyspraxiafoundation.org.uk	The Dyspraxia Foundation has a useful fact sheet on Verbal Dyspraxia
www.stammeringcentre.org	Providing advice on childhood stammering
www.nas.org.uk	Support and advice for anyone interested in autism and autistic spectrum difficulties
www.makaton.org	Resources and information about MAKATON signing
www.ndcs.org.uk	National Deaf Children's Society provides information on hearing difficulties